are available to read at

Forgotten Books

www.ForgottenBooks.com

Forgotten Books' App
Available for mobile, tablet & eReader

ISBN 978-1-333-94914-3
PIBN 10744725

This book is a reproduction of an important historical work. Forgotten Books uses state-of-the-art technology to digitally reconstruct the work, preserving the original format whilst repairing imperfections present in the aged copy. In rare cases, an imperfection in the original, such as a blemish or missing page, may be replicated in our edition. We do, however, repair the vast majority of imperfections successfully; any imperfections that remain are intentionally left to preserve the state of such historical works.

Forgotten Books is a registered trademark of FB &c Ltd.
Copyright © 2015 FB &c Ltd.
FB &c Ltd, Dalton House, 60 Windsor Avenue, London, SW19 2RR.
Company number 08720141. Registered in England and Wales.

For support please visit www.forgottenbooks.com

1 MONTH OF FREE READING

at

www.ForgottenBooks.com

By purchasing this book you are eligible for one month membership to ForgottenBooks.com, giving you unlimited access to our entire collection of over 700,000 titles via our web site and mobile apps.

To claim your free month visit: www.forgottenbooks.com/free744725

* Offer is valid for 45 days from date of purchase. Terms and conditions apply.

English
Français
Deutsche
Italiano
Español
Português

www.forgottenbooks.com

Mythology Photography **Fiction**
Fishing Christianity **Art** Cooking
Essays Buddhism Freemasonry
Medicine **Biology** Music **Ancient Egypt** Evolution Carpentry Physics
Dance Geology **Mathematics** Fitness
Shakespeare **Folklore** Yoga Marketing
Confidence Immortality Biographies
Poetry **Psychology** Witchcraft
Electronics Chemistry History **Law**
Accounting **Philosophy** Anthropology
Alchemy Drama Quantum Mechanics
Atheism Sexual Health **Ancient History**
Entrepreneurship Languages Sport
Paleontology Needlework Islam
Metaphysics Investment Archaeology
Parenting Statistics Criminology
Motivational

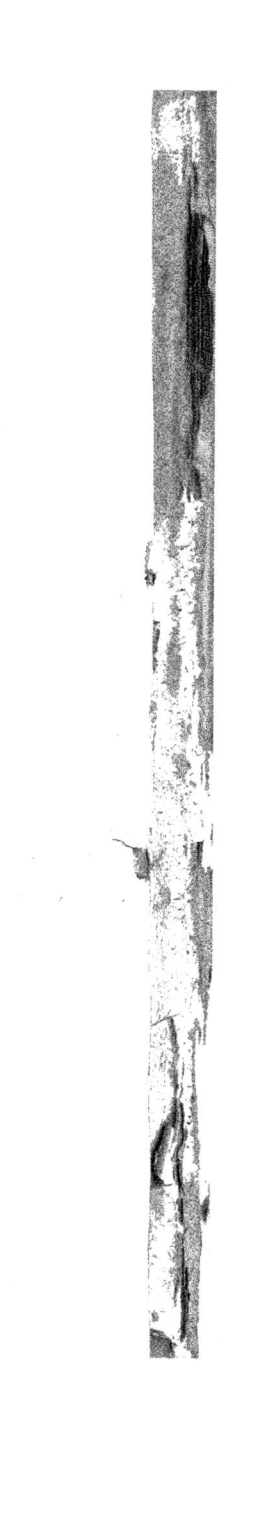

Accession No. 285,225

Added _Nov 3,_ 1880.

Catalogued by

Revised by

MEMORANDA.

A SERIOUS

CALL

IN

CHRISTIAN LOVE

TO ALL

PEOPLE

TO TURN TO THE

SPIRIT OF CHRIST

IN THEMSELVES;

That they may come to have a right understanding of the things of GOD, and be enabled thereby to serve him acceptably:— With some observations on the following heads:

I. THE UNIVERSALITY OF GOD'S LOVE, IN SENDING HIS SON TO DIE FOR ALL MEN.	IV. BAPTISM.
	V. THE SUPPER.
	VI. PERFECTION.
II. THE HOLY SCRIPTURES.	VII. THE RESURRECTION.
III. WORSHIP.	VIII. SWEARING.

1. THES v. 21. *Prove all things, hold fast that which is good.*
ROM. i. 19. *That which may be known of God, is manifest in them.*

PHILADELPHIA:
PRINTED BY JOSEPH CRUKSHANK.
1806.

THE
PREFACE.

FRIENDLY READER,

WHAT *is here presented to thy view, is written in great love, and I desire that the Lord, by his Holy Spirit, may give thee a right understanding of the truths herein laid down.* Our principles and doctrine have been very much misrepresented, and many of our Friends' words and writings have been wrested and misconstrued by many who wanted charity, which is the bond of perfection; the Apostle has excellently described it in his first epistle to the Corinthians; he saith, charity suffereth long, and is kind; charity envieth not; charity vaunteth not itself, is not puffed up, doth not behave itself unseemly, seeketh not her own, is not easily provoked, thinketh no evil, rejoiceth not in iniquity, but rejoiceth in the truth: *Oh, that it might prevail amongst the children of men universally, that so there might be no envying one another: charity is so far from speaking evil, or doing evil, that it thinketh no evil:* Though, *saith the Apostle,* I bestow all my goods to feed the poor, and though I give my body to be burned, and, have not charity, it profiteth me nothing. *It were greatly to be desired, that all would endeavour to excel therein, that so there might be an holy harmony amongst the children of men.*

1 Cor. xiii. 4. 5, 6,

1. Cor. xiii. 3.

THE PREFACE.

This treatise *being small, may come into many hands, where some larger books, that give a more full and particular account of our doctrine and principles, may not come; and if the observations that are made on the several heads touched upon, may have the good effect to remove prejudice, and open the understanding of the religious and well-minded, it will very much answer the desire of him who wishes well to thee, and all men.*

BENJAMIN HOLME.

A SERIOUS

CALL

IN

CHRISTIAN LOVE

TO ALL PEOPLE &c.

AS the Lord hath been so wonderfully gracious and kind to the children of men who were gone astray from him, that he hath sent forth the *Spirit of his Son into their hearts*, to be a guide and teacher to them; it is greatly to be desired, they may all take heed unto it, that thereby they may be enabled to withstand and resist the enemy of their souls, in all his temptations and assaults; for it is certain, as Christ said, *without me ye can do nothing;* we are not able without the help of his spirit, to resist the least temptation; for in that divine light, *which lighteth every man that cometh into the World,* and gives men and women a sight and discovery of that which is evil, there is power to enable them to withstand and resist the enemy in all his temptations, as they take heed to it; but many people are strangers to this divine light, though the apostle *Paul* tells us how men may know it; he saith, *all things that are reproved, are made manifest by the light; for whatsoever doth make manifest is light.* It is *no sin to be tempted,* if men shut out the temptation as soon as it is presented; for we read that Christ was tempted several ways, but

Gal. iv. 6.

John i. 9

Eph. v. 13.

Mat. iv. 1.

he overcame the tempter by resisting of him; the apostle *James* saith, *Resist the Devil, and he will flee from you: draw nigh to God, and he will draw nigh to you.* It is to this holy light and spirit that lets people see the evil when it is presented, that we endeavour to turn the minds of the children of men, that thereby we may be enabled to withstand the enemy in all his temptations; we read, that *The Nations of them which are saved shall walk in the light of the Lamb.* If *we walk in the light*, saith *John, as he is in the light, we have fellowship one with another; and the blood of Jesus Christ his son, cleanseth us from all Sin.* If all that profess to be the followers of the Lord Jesus Christ, did but walk in this holy light as they ought to do, they would shew forth *Christianity* in the purity of it, and adorn the doctrine of God our Saviour, by their good and holy living; we read, *The light shineth in darkness, and the darkness comprehended it not.* How many that are strangers to this holy light which God hath caused to shine in men's dark hearts, have spoken evil of it, and also of many that have borne testimony to it? we read that the apostle *Paul was sent to turn men from darkness to light, and from the power of Satan to God.* And this is the great labour now of those that are truly the ministers of Christ, to turn the Children of men to that true light, which we read, *lighteth every man that cometh into the world.* This divine light ought not to be rejected, nor the true way of worshipping God despised, because they may be evilly spoken of by many that are ignorant of them: The way in which the apostle *Paul* worshipped God was, by some that were strangers to it, counted *Heresy*, and the believers were accounted *a sect every were spoken against*. And it is said concerning Christ, *have any of the rulers or of the* Phari- John vii. 48, sees, *believed on him; but this people who knoweth not* 49. *the law are cursed.* They were so ignorant, that they counted those that believed in Christ accursed. Many of the children of God have been evilly spoken of by those that were strangers to the Lord; *behold* saith *John, what manner of love the Father* 1 John iii. 1, 2, *hath bestowed upon us, that we should be called the Sons of God; therefore the world knoweth us not, because it knew him not.* He assigns the reason why the world knew them not, *because,* saith he, *it knew him not.* While *Saul* was ignorant of God, he persecuted his people; all his learning and scholarship did not give him the knowledge of God, nor yet the knowledge of his people; *and* Saul, *yet breathing out* Acts ix. 1, 2, *threatnings and slaughter against the disciples of the* 3, 7, 5. *Lord, went unto the high-priest, and desired of him letters to* Damascus, *to the synagogues, that if he found any of this way, whether they were men or women, he might bring them bound unto* Jerusalem; *and, as he journeyed, he came near* Damascus, *and suddenly there shined round about him a light from heaven, and he heard a voice saying,* Saul, Saul, *why persecutest thou me? and he said, who art thou Lord? and the Lord said, I am* JESUS *whom thou persecutest; it is hard for thee to kick against the pricks.* It is to be feared, that many do not know that it is the Lord by his Spirit that inwardly pricks them when they do amiss. Now here is the ground of persecution, when men know not God, nor those that are truly his people, they persecute the true worshippers of God as *Hereticks.* How many of the Martyrs in Queen *Mary's* Days were persecuted and put to death as *Hereticks,* by those that were ignorant of God? and how many of *our friends* have been persecuted unto death by those that were strangers to the Lord and to his people? But as it was of old, so it is now, *he that is born after the flesh, persecutes him that is born after the Spirit:* we read how Christ said to his followers, *if the world hate you, ye know that it hated me before it hated you: if ye were of the world, the world would love his own; but because ye are not of the world, but I have chosen you out of the world, therefore the world hateth you: remember the word that I said unto you, the servant is not greater than the Lord: if they have persecuted me, they will also persecute you.* It has often been the lot of many of the followers of Christ, to be persecuted and reviled, and evil spoken of; but our Saviour, to encourage his disciples to bear persecution, and the reproaches and revilings of men, saith, *blessed are ye when men shall revile you, and persecute you, and shall say all manner of evil against you falsly, for my sake; rejoice and be exceeding glad; for great is your reward in heaven; for so persecuted they the prophets which were before you.* Although they that believed in Christ were accounted accursed by some, it was happy for them who did believe in, and receive him, *to them he gave power to become the Sons of God.* This is the great blessing which they have that receive Christ by his Spirit into their hearts; as they are subject to him, they do not only receive power to conquer their lusts and passions, but also to do the will of God, and keep his commands. But how many that are strangers to the inward appearance of the Lord Jesus Christ, by his light and spirit in men's hearts, have looked upon it as strange doctrine to preach Christ *within?* This is *the Mystery which hath been hid from ages and from generations, but now is made manifest to his saints, to whom God*

Gal. iv. 29.

John xv. 18. 19, 20.

Mat. v. 11, 12.

John i 12.

Col. 1. 26. 27.

would make known what is the riches of the glory of of this mystery among the Gentiles, *which is Christ in you the hope of glory.* And when some of *our friends* have borne testimony to that divine light *which lighteth every man that cometh into the world,* many have made a wonder of it, how the light could be in men; and have spoken slightly of the spirit; although we read, *as many as are led by the Spirit of God, they are the Sons of God. If any man* (saith the apostle) *hath not the Spirit of Christ, he is none of his.* If men have not this spirit for their guide, they cannot be Christians, nor members of *Christ's* church, although they may be strict in observing a great many outward observations; for we read, that *in Christ Jesus neither circumcision availeth any thing, nor uncircumcision, but a new creature.* It is as men come to be born of the *divine nature,* being created anew in Christ Jesus unto good works, that they come to have a right understanding of the things of God; *I thank thee, O Father,* (saith Christ) *Lord of heaven and earth, because thou hast hid these things from the wise and prudent, and hast revealed them unto babes; even so, Father, for so it seemed good in thy sight.* He that is truly a child of God, and born of his spirit, has a more true and sensible knowledge of God, and also of the mysteries of his kingdom, than men in their natural and unconverted state can attain unto by all their wisdom and parts; for we read, that *the natural man receiveth not the things of the Spirit of God, for they are foolishness unto him, neither can he know them, because they are spiritually discerned;* they are beyond his reach and comprehension: the apostle saith, *Prove all things; hold fast that which is good.* Now the

John i. 9

Romans viii. 14.
Rom. viii. 9.

Gal. vi. 15.

Mat. xi. 25, 26.

1 Cor. ii. 14.

1 Thes. v. 21.

way for men to have a right and clear discovery of the truth, is to come to that divine light, which God has caused to shine in men's hearts. The apostle saith, *God who commanded the light to shine out of darkness, hath shined in our hearts, to give the light of the knowledge of the glory of God, in the face of Jesus Christ.* And as the Lord, by his light, gives thee a sight and discovery of the truth, I desire that thou mayest embrace it, and join with it; *The Lord,* saith the prophet, *hath shewed thee, O man, what is good: and what doth the Lord require of thee, but to do justly, and to love mercy, and to walk humbly with thy God?* Now the Lord, by his holy light, doth not only shew men that which is good, and what he requires of them; but he is near to shew them that which is evil, in its very first appearance. *He that shews to man his thoughts,* saith the prophet, *the Lord of Hosts is his name:* the apostle saith, *but all things that are reproved are made manifest by the light: for whatsoever doth make manifest is light.* Now this holy light, which gives men a sight and discovery of that which is evil, when it is presented, is the great touch-stone that we desire all may come to. If men do not take heed to this, they may soon err in judgment, and receive and embrace false doctrine, and wrong principles. And men's receiving false and wrong opinions, doth very much open a door for wrong practices. If men once entertain a belief, that there is no possibility of their conquering and overcoming their corruptions while here, what encouragement is there for them to war against them? or if they believe that there is a *Purgatory,* or a place in which they may be cleansed from their sins after death, it is no wonder if they live so as to fulfil and gratify their own carnal desires and

2 Cor. iv. 6.

Micah vi. 8.

Amos. iv. 13.

Ephes. v. 13.

inclinations. But it is his work that was a lyar from the beginning, to persuade men to believe this: we do not read, that the rich man that we have an account of in *Luke,* met with any place of cleansing after death. And if men entertain a belief, that God has before ordained a great part of mankind to perish, and the rest to be saved; and that the numbers are so fixed, that none can be diminished from them that are to perish, or any added to the number of them that are to be saved, what need any body take any care about another world? this doctrine doth very much destroy religion and *Christianity.* I believe some have been so darkened in their understanding, that they have not stuck to say, that God has fore-ordained whatever comes to pass; that he has appointed the murderer to murder, and the thief to steal, that so they might consequently perish. How contrary is this doctrine to what we read in the Holy Scripture, where the Lord has said, *as I live, I have no pleasure in the death of the wicked, but that the wicked turn from his way and live.* Ez. xxxiii. 11. We read, that *they have built the high places of* Tophet, *which is in the Valley of the Son of* Hinnom, *to burn their sons and their daughters in the fire; which* Jer. vii 31 saith the Lord, *I commanded them not, neither came it into my heart.* Although this came to pass, the Lord was so far from ordaining it, that speaking after the manner of men, he said, *it came not into his heart.* It would be abominable to say, that God ordains all the wicked things which come to pass. I wish that all would be careful how they are imposed upon to receive any doctrines which are repugnant to the doctrine of Christ, and the primitive *Christians,* recorded in the Holy Scriptures: and that people would compare their doctrine with the doctrine there laid down, and see how they correspond. It has pleased God to raise up a people to preach the same doctrine, and bear the same testimony, that the apostles and primitive *Christians* bore: *John* saith, *we are of God, he that knoweth God, heareth us: he that is not of God heareth not us.* I desire that none may reject the truth, because it may be held forth by a people that are despised by many that do not rightly know them: *for ye see your calling, brethren, how that not many wise men after the flesh, not many mighty, not many noble, are called; but God hath chosen the foolish things of the world to confound the wise, and God hath chosen the weak things of the world to confound the things which are mighty, and base things of the world, and things which are despised, hath God chosen; yea and things which are not, to bring to nought things that are, that no flesh may glory in his presence.* Although the most of them that believed in and received the Lord Jesus Christ, were not the wise, and mighty, and noble; yet we may conclude safely, that some of the wise, *&c.* did believe in him: and although the generality of them that are now come to believe in, and receive the Lord Jesus Christ in his Spiritual appearance, are not of the wise and noble, yet blessed be the Lord, some such are come to believe in, and receive Christ by his Spirit into their hearts; and that all may thus receive him, is my sincere desire.

I. CONCERNING THE UNIVERSALITY OF GOD'S LOVE, IN SENDING HIS SON TO DIE FOR ALL MEN.

WE freely own, that it is the duty of the children of men to believe in Christ, as he did outwardly appear; and we hold it to be absolutely needful, that they believe his death and sufferings, and what he has done for them, without them, where it has pleased God to afford them the benefit of the Holy Scriptures that declare thereof; yet we believe this outward knowledge is not so absolutely essential to Salvation, but that men may be saved by the Lord Jesus Christ that suffered upon the cross for them, if they are subject to his Spirit in their hearts, although their lots may be cast in those remote parts of the world, where they are without the benefit of the Holy Scriptures, and may know nothing of the coming of Christ in the flesh; for the apostle *Paul*, in the fifth of the *Romans* saith, *as by the offence of one, judgment came upon all men to condemnation, even so by the righteousness of one, the free gift came upon all men, unto justification of life;* for as all men partake of the fruit of *Adam's* fall, by reason of that evil seed, which through him is communicated unto them, which inclines them unto evil, although many thousands of them never heard of the fall of *Adam*, nor of his eating of the forbidden fruit: so we believe many may, and do receive benefit by the Lord Jesus Christ, as they take heed to that divine light and grace, which is communicated to mankind universally, through him, although they may know nothing of his coming in the flesh. Now though we hold it absolutely needful, that men believe in the death and sufferings of Christ, where they have the benefit of the Holy Scriptures, that declare thereof, as is before observed; yet all this knowledge will not entitle to a part in the kingdom of God, unless they know him that died for them, to save them out of those things that unfit them for that holy kingdom, into which nothing that is unclean can enter.

John i. 9.

But because we bear testimony to the inward appearance of the Lord Jesus Christ, by his light and Spirit in men's hearts, some have been so unkind and unjust, that they have not stuck to say, that we denied the Lord Jesus Christ that suffered without the Gates of *Jerusalem* for us; which is a very great abuse upon us; for we firmly believe in him that was born of the virgin *Mary*, that suffered upon the cross for the redemption of mankind universally; and we are so far from denying him that died for us, and rose again and ascended into heaven, and is come again by his Spirit into our hearts, that we hold forth his death and sufferings in a far more extensive manner than many others do; for a great many will have it, that Christ only died for the believers, and a part of mankind; but we believe, according to the Scripture, that he tasted death for every man:

Heb. ii. 9.

but we see Jesus, who was made a little lower than the Angels, for the suffering of death, crowned with glory and honour; that he, by the grace

1 John ii 1, 2

of God, should taste death for every man. My little children, these things write I unto you, that ye sin not; and if any man sin, we have an advocate with the Father, Jesus Christ the righteous; and he is the propitiation for our sins: and not for ours only, but also for the sins of the whole World. Here is the wonderful love of God set forth to mankind universally;

Rom. v. 18.

Therefore, as by the offence of one, judgment came upon all men to condemnation; even so by the righteous-

ness of one, the free gift came upon all men to justification of life. So that the plaister is as broad as the sore. Now although we believe that Christ has, by his offering up of himself once for all, cleared the score, so far, upon the account of infants and mankind in general, that no man will perish because of the sin of *Adam;* yet we do not believe that the death and sufferings of Christ without the gates of *Jerusalem* will render men justified, and acceptable in the sight of God, except they know him that died for them, to redeem them out of actual sinning, and from those things that unfit them for the kingdom of God: *Know ye not,* saith the *apostle, that the unrighteous shall not inherit the kingdom of God? be not deceived; neither fornicators, nor idolaters, nor adulterers, nor effeminate, nor abusers of themselves with mankind, nor thieves, nor covetous, nor drunkards, nor revilers, nor extortioners, shall inherit the kingdom of God. And such were some of you; but ye are washed, but ye are sanctified, but ye are justified in the name of the Lord Jesus and by the Spirit of our God.* Here the apostle has clearly set forth how men are justified. Now this is what we are concerned for, that all people may come to know the Lord to work a change in their hearts, and wash them by his Spirit; *He saved us by the washing of regeneration, and renewing of the Holy Ghost, which he shed on us abundantly, through Jesus Christ our Saviour.* Now here is salvation and justification by Christ upon a true and right foundation; *and she shall bring forth a Son, and thou shalt call his name* JESUS; *for he shall save his people from their sins.* Mark, that salvation from sin is the way for men to be saved by Christ, from the wrath to come; for we read that, *tribulation and an-*

1 Cor. vi, 9, 10, 11.

Titus iii 5, 6.

Mat. i. 2f.

Rom. ii. 9.

guish will be *upon every soul of man that doeth evil;* *of the* Jew *first, and also of the* Gentile. *There is therefore now no condemnation to them which are in Christ Jesus, who walk not after the flesh, but after the Spirit.* As men come to witness a being washed and sanctified, and brought into Christ, and know their abiding to be in him, they are redeemed out of those things that bring condemnation.

If any man be in Christ, he is a new creature, *whosoever abideth in him, sinneth not.* We know *that whosoever is born of God, sinneth not; but he that is begotten of God, keepeth himself, and that wicked one toucheth him not. He that believeth on the Son of God, hath the witness in himself.* This is the sum of all, for men so to live, that they may have the witness in themselves, that they please God. We read concerning *Enoch,* that before he was translated, he had this testimony, that he *pleased God. If our heart condemn us, God is greater than our heart, and knoweth all things: If our heart condemn us not, then have we confidence towards God.* Friendly reader, whoever thou art, that art condemned and reproved in thyself, for that which is evil, I tenderly desire thou mayest turn to that Holy Spirit, which doth inwardly reprove thee for it: *If I go not away, the Comforter will not come unto you; but if I depart, I will send him unto you. And when he is come he will reprove the world of Sin.* The same Holy Spirit that reproves men for sin, will not only give them power over those things that they are overcome with, which are evil, if they take heed unto it; but as they come out of those things they are reproved for, it will be a divene comforter to them, and they will be inwardly justified in themselves. We read that *the grace of God that bringeth salvation hath appeared to all men, teaching us, that denying ungodliness, and worldly lusts, we should live soberly, righteously, and godly in this present world; looking for that blessed hope, and the glorious appearing of the great God, and our Saviour Jesus Christ; who gave himself for us, that he might redeem us from all iniquity, and purify unto himself a peculiar people, zealous of good works.* Now although the apostle has here so excellently borne testimony to the sufficiency and universality of the grace of God, many are so narrow, that they are not willing to own, that Christ has died for all; nor will they allow that saving grace is given to all, although we read, that *a manifestation of the Spirit is given to every man to profit withal.* 1. Cor. xii. And in the parable of the *sower*, that went forth to sow, the seed fell on all the four sorts of ground, but it did not bring forth fruit to perfection, save only in the good ground; and the unprofitable servant had a talent committed to him, which was sufficient for him, if he had but improved it; it is plain, that the fault was in himself; so that if any man perish, he is the cause of his own destruction; as it was said of *Israel*, O Israel, *thou hast destroyed thyself! but in me is thy help.* Hosea xiii. 9. God gave them of his good Spirit to instruct them, but they rebelled against him. Nehem. ix. 20. Many, for want of a right understanding, have made a very wrong use of *Paul's* words in the ninth of the *Romans*; *for the children being not yet born, neither having done any good or evil, that the purpose of God according to election might stand, not of works, but of him that calleth, it was said unto her, the elder shall serve the younger. As it is written,* Jacob *have I loved, but* Esau *have I hated.* Rom. ix. 11, 12, 13. Now the apos-

C

tle doth not say, that before the children were born, it was said, *Jacob* have I loved, and *Esau* have I hated; but that *the elder shall serve the younger;* and *as it is written,* Jacob *have I loved, but* Esau *have I hated:* he has reference to what is written: read *Obadiah; for thy violence against thy brother* Jacob, *shame shall cover thee, and thou shalt be cut off for ever.* If God had hated *Esau,* and ordained *Pharaoh* to perish, before they were born, he would have been a respecter of persons, which is contrary to the apostle *Peter's* testimony; *of a truth, I perceive,* said he, *that God is no respecter of persons, but in every nation he that feareth him, and worketh righteousness, is accepted with him.* Here are the conditions laid down, upon which all people may be accepted of God; for we believe, as it is the will of God that all men should be saved, so he gives to every man a day of visitation, in which he inwardly strives with them, by his Holy Spirit, to reclaim them. He strove long with the people in the old world; *and the* Lord *said, my Spirit shall not always strive with man, for that he also is flesh.* There was a time in which they might have been saved, but they would not be reclaimed from those things that were displeasing to him, therefore he cut them off in his wrath; and there was also a time in which the inhabitants of *Jerusalem* might have been gathered, but they would not, and our Saviour wept over them, and said, O Jerusalem! Jerusalem! *thou that killest the prophets, and stonest them which are sent unto thee, how often would I have gathered thy children together, even as a hen gathereth her chickens under her wings, and ye would not? behold your house is left unto you desolate!* Christ did not say,

Obad. i. 10.

Acts x. 34, 35.

Gen. vi. 3.

Mat. xxiii. 37, 38.

they could not be gathered, but said, *ye would not*; so that the cause why they were not gathered, was not in the Lord, but in themselves: but if God, by a secret decree, had beforehand determined their destruction, why should he have sent his servants to them, in order that they might be gathered? and what will people make of our Saviour's weeping over them, if they were before ordained inevitably to perish? I wish all may consider these things seriously; the apostle saith, *what if God, willing to shew* Rom. ix. 22. *his wrath, and to make his power known, endured with much long-suffering the vessels of wrath fitted to destruction?* and why is this long suffering, but in order that they might be gained upon? why was *the long-suffering of God, which waited in the days* 1 Pet. iii. 20. *of Noah, while the Ark was preparing*, but that they might be reclaimed from their wrong doings? when *Pharaoh* had refused to let *Israel* go, and said, *who is the Lord, that I should obey his voice,* Exod. v. 2. *to let* Israel *go? I know not*, said he, *the Lord, neither will I let* Israel *go;* then we read that the Lord said, *I will harden* Pharaoh's *heart, and multiply my signs* Exod. vii. 3. *and my wonders in the land of* Egypt. And the Lord shewed his power in his destruction, as he Exod. xiv. 23. did in the destruction of the old world: but let it be considered, that they brought this upon themselves, by their rebelling against him; for why should the Lord have striven with the old world, if he had determined their destruction before hand? friendly reader, I desire the Lord may open thy understanding by his Holy Spirit, that thou mayst have a right discerning of these things; *Peter* saith, *account that the long-suffering of our Lord is* 2 Pet. iii. 15, *salvation, even as our beloved brother* Paul *also, according to the wisdom given unto him, hath written* 16.

unto you; as also in all his Epistles, speaking in them of these things; in which are some things hard to be understood, which they that are unlearned and unstable, wrest, as they do also the other Scriptures, unto their own destruction. Peter did not mean that it was those that were outwardly unlearned, that wrested *Paul's* words; for we read, that he and *John* were both said to be unlearned and ignorant men; *Now when they saw the boldness of* Peter *and* John, *and perceived that they were unlearned and ignorant men, they marvelled; and they took knowledge of them, that they had been with Jesus.* It was then, and is now, such as are unlearned in the School of Christ, that did and do wrest *Paul's* words; and if people do not come to learn of Christ, it is no wonder if they put wrong and gross constructions upon many places of the Holy Scriptures; but although this place hath been made very ill use of by many, the apostle *Paul* doth give ample and full testimony of the good will of God to mankind; *I exhort,* saith he, *therefore, that first of all, supplications, prayers, intercessions, and giving of thanks, be made for all men; for kings, and for all that are in authority; that we may lead a quiet and peaceable life, in all godliness and honesty; for this is good and acceptable in the sight of God our Saviour, who will have all men to be saved, and to come unto the knowledge of the truth.* If the apostle had believed, that a part of mankind were ordained to perish, before they were born, he would not have advised *Timothy* to pray for all men, nor have told him, that it was the will of God that all men should be saved; so that if any man perish, as is before observed, the fault is in himself; *say unto them, as I live, saith the Lord God, I have no pleasure in the*

Acts vi. 13.

1 Tim. ii. 1, 2, 3, 4.

Ezek. xxxiii. 11, 13, 14, 15.

death of the wicked; but that the wicked turn from his way and live. When I shall say to the righteous, that he shall surely live; if he trust to his own righteousness, and commit iniquity, all his righteousness shall not be remembered; but for his iniquity that he hath committed, he shall die for it. Again, when I say unto the wicked, thou shalt surely die; if he turn from his sin, and do that which is lawful and right; if the wicked restore the pledge, give again that he had robbed, walk in the statutes of life, without committing iniquity, he shall surely live, he shall not die. I wish that all might seriously consider this, and that all who think they stand and are secure, may take heed lest they fall; and that they who have gone into evil things, may be encouraged to turn to the Lord, by true repentance and amendment of life, that they may find mercy at his hand, as the prophet saith, *let the wicked forsake his way, and the unrigh-* Isa. lv. 7. *teous man his thoughts; and let him return unto the Lord, and he will have mercy upon him, and to our God, for he will abundantly pardon.* We are not of their mind that say, *once in grace and ever in grace,* or that the least degree of true and saving grace cannot be fallen from: but we believe men may now, as some of old did, make shipwreck of faith and of a good conscience; and from what is before said it is plain, that a righteous man may turn from his righteousness, therefore it is good for all to be watchful; *what I say unto you,* said Christ to his Mark xiii. 37. followers, *I say unto all, watch.* No man is longer safe than whilst he is upon his watch. It was when *David* and *Peter* were off their watch, that they fell, and the miscarriages that are among the children of men, are owing to their unwatchfulness · not but that we believe the grace and good Spirit of God is sufficient to keep men from falling and sinning, and out of all evil and hurtful things, as they take heed unto it; unto which grace, friendly reader, I commend thee for safety and preservation.

2. CONCERNING THE HOLY SCRIPTURES.

ALTHOUGH some have misrepresented us, as though we undervalued or disesteemed the Holy Scriptures of the old and new Testament, yet we do bless the Lord, and have great cause so to do, that the excellent counsel therein contained, which proceeded from the Spirit of God, is preserved upon record to this day; and it is a great favour that we live under a Government, where we have the liberty to read them, this being a privilege that many called *Christians* are deprived of, in some other countries; and I wish that all would be frequent in reading of them: The apostle *Paul* commended *Timothy*, in that *from a child he had known the Holy Scriptures, which,* saith he, *are able to make thee wise unto Salvation, through faith, which is in Christ Jesus. All Scripture, given by inspiration of God, is profitable for doctrine, for reproof, for correction, for instruction in righteousness, that the man of God may be perfect, thoroughly furnished unto all good works.* Search the Scriptures, saith Christ, *for in them ye think ye have eternal life, and they are they which testify of me, and ye will not come to me that ye might have life.* They are greatly to be valued, in that they testify of Christ, in whom there is power to give men victory over their corruptions and passions, and enable them to do

2 Tim. iii. 15, 16, 17.

John v. 39, 40.

the will of God. We read that Christ *came unto his*   John i. 11, 12. *own, and his own received him not ; but as many as received him, to them gave he power to become the sons of God.* They that receive Christ by his Spirit into their hearts, they receive power; for Christ's Spirit is a *Christian's* strength: *I can do all things,*   Phil. iv. 13. saith the apostle, *through Christ, which strengtheneth me.* We read, that *no prophecy of the Scripture*   2 Peter i. 20, 21. *is of any private interpretation ; for the prophecy came not in old time by the will of man ; but holy men of God spake as they were moved by the Holy Ghost.* Now we say, the most true interpreter of the Holy Scripture, is the Holy Ghost, or Spirit, from which they did proceed; we read, that *the natural man*   1 Cor. ii. 14. *receives not the things of the Spirit of God, neither can he know them,* saith the text, and there is a strong reason laid down for it, *because they are spiritually discerned ;* they are beyond his reach and comprehension ; *For what man knoweth the things*   1 Cor. ii. 11. *of a man, save the spirit of a man which is in him; even so the things of God knoweth no man, but the Spirit of God.* This is the key which opens the mysteries of the kingdom of God to men : I take this to be the great reason why there are such great mistakes about religion, and why many put such gross constructions upon many parts of the Holy Scriptures, 'as they do, because they do not come to that divine Spirit which gives a right and true understanding; as *Elihu* said, *there is a spirit in man, and the inspiration of the Almighty giveth them understanding.* Till   Job. xxxii. 8. men come to the Holy Spirit of God in themselves, they can neither know God, nor the things of God; for we read, that *no man knoweth the Father save the Son and he to whomsoever the Son will reveal him.*   Mat. 11, 27. Now if revelation was ceased, as some do imagine it is, what a sad condition would mankind be in? for we read, *the world by wisdom knows not God;* there is no knowledge of God, but by the revelation of his Son; and it is as men come to have an inward knowledge of God, that they come to have a right understanding of the Holy Scriptures, which proceeded from the good Spirit of God; wherefore we highly value them; though it is to be feared, some called *Christians* do disbelieve many of the great truths therein contained; for I believe that a man, through often rebelling against the Holy Spirit of God in himself, may arrive to such a degree of wickedness, that he may reject the Scriptures, and count them but fables; and may be so far from owning of any thing of God in man, as to deny the Lord that bought him, and, according to *Psalm* xiv. 1. he may say in his heart, *there is no God.* It is the work of the enemy of all righteousness, to persuade men there is no God, and that the Scriptures are but a fiction, and that men are not accountable for their words or actions, and that there are no future rewards and punishments; that they might walk at large, and take their full swing in wickedness. It is greatly to be desired, if there be any such now living, whose day of mercy is not wholly over, that have arrived to such a degree of hardness and wickedness as this is, that they may be brought to a sense of their iniquity and error, and be so truly humbled in soul because thereof, that, if possible, they might find mercy at the Lord's hand. The better *Christian* that any man is, the more true and real value he has for the Holy Scriptures.

1 Cor. i. 21.

3. CONCERNING WORSHIP.

WE live in a time in which there is great difference even among those called *Christians*, about religion and the worship of God. Difference about religion and the worship of God is no new thing; the *Jews* and *Samaritans* differed to such a degree, that it seems they did not deal with one another. It is very much amiss, where religion sours people, and makes them rigid, and bitter one against another. *Christianity* is *love*, and he that is a *Christian* in his heart, is full of pity and good will to them that are under a mistake in matters of religion; and the worst that he wishes for all such, is, that the Lord may direct them right; for they that have the mind of Christ, would not have any soul to err, either in faith or practice. Our Saviour, in his discourse with the woman of *Samaria*, has clearly described the true and spiritual worship; *But the hour cometh and now is, when the true worshippers shall worship the Father in Spirit and in truth; for the Father seeketh such to worship him. God is a Spirit, and they that worship him, must worship him in spirit and in truth.* Now, we believe, that as God is a Spirit, he may be truly worshipped, as we are gathered in his Spirit, though there be not a word outwardly spoken among us; as Christ said, *where two or three are gathered together in my name, there am I in the midst of them;* and the holy prophet saith, *they that wait upon the Lord, shall renew their strength: they shall mount up with wings as eagles; they shall run and not be weary; and they shall walk, and not faint.* Although I believe a great many

John iv. 9.

John iv. 23, 24.

Mat. xviii. 20.

Isa. xl. 31.

pious good Christians can say, as they have waited humbly upon the Lord, in true silence of all flesh, with their minds truly staid upon him, they have enjoyed that divine comfort which has been beyond what they could express in words; yet this of *silent waiting* is a great mystery to many people. There is a divine teacher near men, even in their own hearts, which is sufficient to teach them, as they take heed thereto. It is to be feared, that many people too much depend upon the teachings of men, and neg-

1 John ii. 27. lect the divine teacher in themselves; *but the anointing which ye have received of him, abideth in you; and ye need not that any man teach you, but as the same anointing teacheth you of all things, and is truth, and is no lie; and even as it hath taught you, ye shall abide in him.* Now we understand the holy man here, to speak in a large sense; he told them, that they needed not that any man taught them, but as the same anointing taught them, &c. We do very much own outward preaching and praying, where it proceeds from this divine anointing. If it please God to speak by this through any instruments, whether male or female, we believe there should be liberty amongst us, for every one to speak as he requires it of them; *for ye may all*

1 Cor. xiv. 31. *prophesy one by one, that all may learn, and all may*
32 *be comforted; and the spirits of the prophets are subject to the prophets. And they were all filled with*

Acts ii. 4. *the Holy Ghost, and began to speak with other tongues, as the Spirit gave them utterance.* We believe the true preaching and praying, is that

Rom. viii. 26. which proceeds from the Holy Spirit; *we know not what we should pray for as we ought, but the Spirit itself maketh intercession for us, with groanings*

Cor. xiv. 15. *which cannot be uttered. I will pray with the Spirit,*

and I will pray with the understanding also; I will sing with the Spirit, and I will sing with the understanding also.

This is the preaching, and praying, and singing, which we own, that is by the direction and assistance of the Holy Spirit. Now some being against women's *speaking* in the church, urge what the apostle saith, *let your women keep silence in the churches, for it is not permitted unto them to speak; but they are commanded to be under obedience, as also saith the law. And if they will learn any thing, let them ask their husbands at home; for it is a shame for women to speak in the church. Let the women learn in silence with all subjection; but I suffer not a woman to teach, nor to usurp authority over the man, but to be in silence.* We do not take this to be a prohibiting holy women to speak, whom the Lord calls thereto; and I think it would be very much amiss to say, that the apostle *Paul* was against holy women speaking, whom God called to speak; but such troublesome and unruly women as disturbed the church by their questions, and usurped authority over the man, which he was against, we are against. If the apostle *Paul* had been against holy women praying and prophesying, why should he lay down a rule how they ought to behave themselves when they pray or prophesy? *but every woman that prayeth or prophesieth with her head uncovered, dishonoureth her head.* And he commends to the believers divers good women. *I commend unto you Phebe our sister, which is a servant of the church.* All good ministers of Jesus Christ are servants to the church. And he advised his true yoke-fellow, *to help those women which laboured with him in the Gospel;* so that he was an encourager of holy wo-

1 Cor. xiv. 34, 35.

1 Tim. ii. 11, 12.

1 Cor. xi. 5.

Rom. xvi. 1 to 13.

Philip iv. 3.

men that laboured, in the Gospel: we read, that *Anna spoke in the temple, and she was a widow of about fourscore and four years, which departed not from the temple, but served God with fastings and prayers, night and day. And she, coming in that instant, gave thanks likewise unto the Lord, and spake of him to all them that looked for redemption in* Jerusalem. And we read, that *Philip* the evangelist had four daughters, virgins, and they did all prophesy. And *Joel* also prophesied that God would pour forth of his Spirit, *&c. But this is that,* saith *Peter, which was spoken by the prophet* Joel; *and it shall come to pass in the last days, saith God, I will pour out of my Spirit upon all flesh: and your sons and your daughters shall prophesy, and your young men shall see visions, and your old men shall dream dreams; and on my servants, and on my handmaids, I will pour out in those days of my Spirit, and they shall prophesy.* Now although prophesying is several times taken in the Scripture for foretelling things to come; read *Jeremiah,* and several other prophecies of the prophets; yet it is also taken for edifying the church; *but he that prophesieth, speaketh unto men to edification, and exhortation, and comfort. He that speaketh in an unknown tongue, edifieth himself; but he that prophesieth, edifieth the church. Mary* was sent by Christ to declare of his resurrection, *Jesus saith unto her, touch me not, for I am not yet ascended to my Father; but go to my brethren, and say unto them, I ascend unto my Father and your Father, and to my God and your God.* And the woman of *Samaria* was instrumental to bring many of her neighbours to believe in Christ; she said, *come see a man which told me all that ever I did: is not this the Christ? and many of the Samaritans of* *that city believed on him, for the saying of the woman, which testified, he told me all that ever I did.* Now it is to Christ, as he inwardly appears in men's hearts by his light and Spirit, that we desire all may come. It is he that shews men when they do amiss. Christ within, *which is the hope of the saints glory,* is a great mystery to many people. *When it pleased God,* saith the apostle *Paul, to reveal his Son in me, that I might preach him among the* Heathen ; *immediately I conferred not with flesh and blood :* here was the Son of God revealed in him. Now that all may have a right understanding of the things of God, we desire that they may come to him that hath the key of *David,* that opens the mysteries of the kingdom of God to men.

Col. 1, 27.

Gal. i. 15. 16.

4. CONCERNING BAPTISM.

BECAUSE of our disuse of water-baptism, and bread and wine, we have been very hardly spoke of, as though we denied the ordinances of Jesus Christ; whereas there is no people that I know of, that do more truly own the necessity of believing and being baptized than we do ; but we do not understand it to be only an historical belief of the conception and birth, and life and miracles, and also of the death and sufferings, and resurrection and ascension of Christ, or a being outwardly baptized with water, that will entitle men to Salvation ; for we read, *that* Simon *the sorcerer believed, and was baptized,* and yet he was so far from being in a state of Salvation, that *Peter* saith to him, *I perceive that thou art in the gall of bitterness, and*

Acts. viii. 13, 23.

in the bond of iniquity. But lest any should be under a mistake, and take the baptism of water to be the one essential and saving baptism, hear the apostle *Peter ; when once the long-suffering of God waited in the days of* Noah, *while the Ark was preparing, wherein few,* that is, *eight souls were saved by water. The* antitype *whereof, even baptism, doth also now save us ; not the putting away the filth of the flesh,* [mark that] *but the answer of a good conscience towards God, by the resurrection of Jesus Christ.* Now it is the baptism of Christ, by his Spirit, that brings men to that ; for it is plain, from the instance of *Simon* before noted, that a man may believe, and be baptized with water, and be so far from having the answer of a good conscience, that he may be in the *Gall of bitterness and in the bond of iniquity,* which is the very reverse of *Christianity.* A great many take the commission in the 28th of *Matthew,* to be a commission for water-baptism ; *go ye, therefore, and teach all nations, baptizing them in the name of the Father, and of the Son, and of the Holy Ghost.* Now here is no mention of water. Is it not reasonable to suppose, that if our dear Lord had intended that they should baptize with water, that he would have expressly mentioned it. Although the apostle *Paul* was not inferior to the chief of the apostles, he saith, *I thank God that I baptized none of you, but* Crispus *and* Gaius ; *lest any should say, that I had baptized in mine own name; and I baptized also the houshold of* Stephanas; *besides, I know not whether I baptized any other; for Christ sent me* NOT *to baptize, but to preach the* Gospel. So that what he did in that case, was by way of condescension, as in the case of circumcising *Timothy,* and going into the temple, and purifying himself. It

Marginal references:
1 Pet. iii. 20, 21.
Mat. xxviii. 19.
1 Cor. i. 14, 15, 16, 17.
Acts. xvi. 3 & xxi. 26.

would be a weak thing to plead for these things now, because the apostle practised them. Doth it therefore follow, that water-baptism should be practised now, because the apostle *Paul*, by way of condescension, practised it? for if he took that commission, *Mat.* xxviii. 19. to be a commission for him to baptize with outward water, we may safely conclude, that he would not have thanked God that he had done him so little service. We do not deny, but that some other of the apostles did also, by way of condescension, practise water-baptism; but that they were commanded to baptize with water in that commission, I think will be too hard for any body to prove. It is possible some [Mat. xxviii. 19.] may be ready to say, it must needs be meant of water; because, say they, no man can baptize with the Spirit, or into the power and Spirit of Christ: we freely own, that no man, as he is a man, by his own power, can do this; neither can any man by his own power, as he is man, *heal the sick, cleanse the* [Mat. x. 8.] *lepers, raise the dead, cast out devils;* and yet we find the disciples were commanded to do these things. And by the same power, by which they did cast out many devils, and healed the sick, *&c.* they were instrumental to baptize men into the name and power of Christ. *And I as began to speak,* saith [Acts xi. 15, 16.] *Peter, the Holy Ghost fell on them, as on us at the beginning. Then remembered I the word of the Lord, how that he said,* John *indeed baptized with water, but ye shall be baptized with the Holy Ghost.* At the great meeting we read of in the second of *Acts,* verse the 4th, it is said, *they were all filled with the Holy Ghost, and began to speak with other tongues as the Spirit gave them utterance;* yet some of the multitude mocked, and were so ignorant of the operation of the Holy Ghost, that they said, verse 13, *these men are full of new wine;* but Peter standing up with the eleven, lifted up his voice, and said unto them, ye men of Judah, *and all ye that dwell at Jerusalem, be this known unto you, and hearken to my words; for these are not drunken, as ye suppose, seeing it is but the third hour of the day. But this is that which was spoken of by the prophet* Joel, &c. It is hard to make men sensible of the operation of the Holy Ghost, and of the Spiritual baptism, while they are strangers to the Spirit in themselves; but if it could be proved, that the disciples, in that commission, were commanded to baptize with or in water, which I believe cannot be done; how will they that are for the sprinkling of infants, prove their practice from that commission, *go teach all nations,* &c. for they are not capable of being taught. As to what is urged of the jailor, and all his, and whole families being baptized; there is no account that there were any infants baptized in any of them. There is abundance of families now, as (we may reasonably suppose) there were then, in which there are no little children. As to that of our Saviour, where he saith, *suffer little children, and forbid them not, to come unto me, for of such is the kingdom,* it cannot be proved from Scripture, that he baptized any of them in, or with water. But as to this practice of sprinkling infants, it is so much without foundation in the Scripture, that a great many people, who are not of our society, do not hold it or own it. The way rightly to understand this commission, is to come to that Spirit by which it was given forth. Many urge, that our Saviour was baptized of *John*; he was also circumcised; doth it therefore follow that we must be circumcised, because he was circumcised? For as he was born under the law, he fulfilled the law, *and he is the end of the law for righteousness-* Rom. x. 4. *sake, to all them that believe.* When Christ came to *John* to be baptized of him, *John,* forbade him, saying, *I have need to be baptized of thee.* Here, *John* Mat. iii. 13, 14. the baptist, who was the administrator of water-baptism, was sensible that he had need to be baptized of Christ, with the baptism of the Holy Ghost: *Suffer it to be so now,* said Christ, *for thus* Verse 15. *it becometh us to fulfil all righteousness*: so that he fulfilled the righteousness of *John's* dispensation. *John* has very clearly and excellently distinguished his baptism of water, from the baptism of Christ, with the Holy Ghost; *I indeed baptize you with wa-* Mat. iii. 11, 12. *ter unto repentance, but he that cometh after me, is mightier than I, whose shoes I am not worthy to bear; he shall baptize you with the Holy Ghost and with fire: whose fan is in his hand, and he will thoroughly purge his floor, and gather his wheat into the garner, but he will burn up the chaff with unquenchable fire.* This is the messenger of the covenant, the prophet speaks of. *The Lord whom ye seek, shall suddenly* Mal iii. 1, 2, 3. *come to his temple; even the messenger of the covenant, whom ye delight in; behold he shall come, saith the Lord of Hosts; but who may abide the day of his coming, and who shall stand when he appeareth? for he is like a refiner's fire, and like fuller's soap: and he shall sit as a refiner and purifier of silver, and he shall purify the sons of* Levi, *and purge them as gold and silver, that they may offer unto the Lord an offering in righteousness.* For this end the Lord Jesus Christ is come into the hearts of men, by his Spirit, to purge them from their dross, and wash them

E

from their uncleanness, that so they may be fitted for that kingdom, into which nothing that is unclean can enter. This is the washing which will avail, for men to know their hearts to be washed from wickedness; as it was said to *Jerusalem, wash thy heart from wickedness.* The apostle *Paul* in his epistle to the *Ephesians* saith, there is *one Lord, one faith, one baptism.* John, as is before observed, has distinguished very plainly between his baptism with water, and the baptism of Christ with the Holy Ghost. Now what we desire is, that all might come to the baptism of the Spirit, which the apostle and primitive *Christians* witnessed, who could say, *by one Spirit are we all baptized into one body, whether we be Jews or Gentiles, whether we be bond or free; and have been all made to drink into one Spirit:* (this is the one baptism.) *For as many of you as have been baptized into Christ, have put on Christ.* Now this is the sum of all, for men to put on the Lord Jesus Christ, the new and heavenly man; then they will witness inward communion with the Lord.

<small>Eph. iv. 5.</small>

<small>1 Cor. xii. 13.</small>

<small>Gal. iii. 27.</small>

But why are many of our sober neighbours so strenuous for water-baptism, and yet neglect to wash one another's feet; when, as we read, *John* xiii. verse 1, to 14, that our Saviour washed the disciples' feet; and he told them, that he had given them an example, that as he had done to them, so they should do to one another: Now here is both example and precept for this; and if we ask many sober people, why they are not in the practice of this, I persume many would be ready to answer, that they look upon it to be but an outward and visible sign, by which our Saviour shewed his followers that they ought to serve one another, and be ready to do the meanest offices of love, if need require: and that they do not hold the ceremonious part of washing one another's feet to be obligatory upon them, as long as they come to the Spiritual part of what was thereby signified, although we find that this was practised by our Saviour. Now why they should lay such stress upon water-baptism, which we cannot find was ever practised by our Saviour, and drop this, deserves their serious consideration: but as we disuse water-baptism, so we do also disuse the ceremonious part of washing one another's feet, being sensible, that they who are come to the spiritual part of what was thereby signified, are come to the end of the outward and visible signs.

5. CONCERNING THE SUPPER.

ALTHOUGH we disuse the outward bread and wine, we do very truly own the spiritual supper of the Lord, which is spoken of in the *Revelations*. *Behold I stand at the door and knock; if* Rev iii. 20. *any man hear my voice, and open the door, I will come in to him, and will sup with him, and he with me.* It is what we desire, that all religious well-minded people, who conscientiously receive the outward bread and wine, may open the door of their hearts, and receive the Lord Jesus Christ by his Spirit, that so they may know an inward supping with him in his kingdom: for we read, *the kingdom of God cometh not with observation, neither shall* Luke xvii. 20. *they say, lo here, or lo there, for behold the king-* 21. *dom of God is within you.* *I will not leave you com-* John xiv. 18. *fortless,* (said Christ our Lord) *I will come to you.*
But I say unto you, I will not drink henceforth of this Mat. xxvi. 29.

fruit of the vine, until that day when I drink it new with you in my Father's kingdom. *He dwelleth with you, and shall be in you.* And in that excellent prayer, he saith to his Father, *I in them, and thou in me, that they may be made perfect in one, and that the world may know that thou hast sent me, and hast loved them, as thou hast loved me.* We bear testimony to the coming of Christ by his spirit into men's hearts; and they that have known him to wash them thoroughly by the water of regeneration, will know inward communion with the Lord, as the good *Christians* of old knew; *that which we have seen, and heard, declare we unto you, that ye also may have fellowship with us; and truly our fellowship is with the Father, and with his Son Jesus Christ.* They were people of blessed experience; and it is what we desire, that the children of men might come to witness this in themselves; for they that are come to have fellowship with the Father, and with the Son, are come to the end of the outward bread and wine, even to the glory of the gospel dispensation, which is a dispensation of enjoyment: for as men are inwardly reconciled, and brought into favour with God, they come to know a feeding on that divine and living bread which comes down from Heaven; *I am* (said Christ) *the living bread which came down from heaven; if any man eat of this bread, he shall live for ever; and the bread that I will give, is my flesh, which I will give for the life of the world. He that eateth my flesh, and drinketh my blood, dwelleth in me, and I in him.* It is as men witness this, that they can speak from their own experience, what a blessed thing it is to have inward communion with Christ. It is the great blessing of wisdom's children, that she brings them to the substance; *I lead in the way of righteousness, in the midst of the paths of judgment, that I may cause those that love me to inherit substance; and I will fill their treasures.* Pro. viii. 20, 21. Reader, this is what is desired for thee, that thou mayest come to the substance, that so thou mayest know a feeding on that divine and spiritual bread which can only satisfy the soul, and a drinking of the wine of the kingdom; but it is hard to make the natural man sensible of these things; they are beyond his reach and comprehension. When our Saviour told *Nicodemus,* that *except a man be born again, he cannot see the kingdom of God:* John iii. 3, 4. Nicodemus *saith unto him, how can a man be born when he is old; can he enter the second time into his mother's womb, and be born?* Notwithstanding that he was a ruler of the *Jews,* he argued very grossly; and how many, when we have borne testimony to the inward appearance of the Lord Jesus Christ, by his light and Spirit in men's hearts, have made very strange of it, and been ready to say, how can this be? and when we have spoken of men's having inward fellowship with the Father, and with the Son, while they are upon the earth, many cannot understand how this can be, although the primitive *Christians* had it in their own experience, as is before observed. The apostle saith, *neither circumcision availeth any thing, nor uncircumcision, but a new creature.* Gal. vi. 15. It doth not avail in the sight of God, whether a man be baptized with water, or not baptized with water; or whether he receives the bread and wine or doth not receive it, if he be not a new creature; we read, *If any man be in Christ, he is a new creature;* 2 Cor. v. 17. and as is before observed, *except a man be born again, he cannot see the kingdom of God.* We greatly desire that all people might have this in their own experience, that so they might walk as becomes the children of God, and manifest themselves to be the followers and disciples of Christ, by their living agreeably to his doctrine; for I count that is the greatest outward visible sign, that any man can give, that he is truly a *Christian,* and a member of Christ's church, for him to live agreeably to the doctrine of Christ; *by this,* said our Saviour, *shall all men know that ye are my disciples, if ye love one another.* Now, to love one another, to love our enemies, to do good for evil, to forgive injuries, to be just and merciful, and walk humbly, as *Christians* ought to do, are good outward visible signs; but we believe no outward observations will make men *Christians,* and members of that pure church which Christ came to present to God, without spot or wrinkle; or any such thing, (but that it should be holy and without blemish) if they do not know the Lord to work a change in their hearts, and redeem them out of those things which unfit them for his holy kingdom; the apostle saith, *He is not a* Jew *that is one outwardly, neither is that circumcision which is outward in the flesh; but he is a* Jew *which is one inwardly, and circumcision is that of the heart in the Spirit, and not of the letter, whose praise is not of men, but of God.* As a man's being outwardly circumcised, and observing a great many *Jewish* rites and ceremonies, did not make him a true and real *Jew,* if he was not one in his heart; so it may be truly said, he is not a *Christian,* that is only one outwardly, although he has been outwardly baptized, and received the bread and wine, and observed a great many outward observations. If he is not one in his heart, all his outward obser-

[margin: John xiii. 35.]
[margin: Eph. v. 27.]
[margin: Rom. ii. 28, 29.]

vations will not render him acceptable in the sight of God. What availed all the *Jews* outward observations while they lived in those things that displeased the Lord ? *Hé that killeth an ox, is as if he slew a man ; he that sacrificeth a lamb, as if he cut off a dog's neck; he that offereth an oblation, as if he offered swine's blood ; he that burneth incense, as if he blessed an idol : yea, they have chosen their own ways, and their soul delighteth in their abominations. I also will choose their delusions, and will bring their fears upon them, because when I called none did answer ; when I spake they did not hear ; but they did evil before mine eyes, and chose that in which I delighted not.* Ifa. lxvi. 3, 4. Here is the reason laid down why the Lord was angry with them. These things afford great instruction and caution ; and I desire that all may learn from what such brought upon themselves, through their choosing their own ways, and delighting in their abominations, to beware of doing the like; but they that are Christ's, and *Christians* in reality, are crucified to the world, with the affections and lusts thereof; and we desire that all who are called *Christians*, may demonstrate themselves to be such, by their so doing, that they may witness the spiritual communion and supper here spoken of. There are many religious people, particularly in *Holland*, who do not profess to be of our society ; though they do not clearly see beyond the use of water-baptism, and bread and wine, do join with us in opposing *swearing* upon any account ; because they are convinced that *all swearing* is forbidden by Christ : *but I say unto you, swear not at all ; neither by heaven, for it is* God's *throne ; nor by the earth, for it is his foot stool ; neither by* Jerusalem, *for it is the* Mat. v. 34, 35, 36, 37.

City of the great King; neither shalt thou swear by thy head, because thou canst not make one hair, white or black; but let your communication be yea, yea; nay, nay; for whatsoever is more than these cometh of evil. And the apostle *James* saith, *but above all things, my brethren, swear not; neither by heaven, nor by the earth, neither by any other oath; but let your yea, be yea; and your nay, nay; lest you fall into condemnation.* They are also one with us in opposing *fighting*, because they look upon it to be contrary to his doctrine, that taught his followers to love their enemies; *But I say unto you, love your enemies, bless them that curse you, do good to them that hate you, and pray for them that despitefully use you, and persecute you.* They are of our minds, that the *ministry should be free*; for they look upon it to be contrary to Christ's doctrine, for men to preach for hire, and worldly ends, who said to his ministers, *freely ye have received, freely give;* and they are likewise one with us, in holding forth the *universal* love of God to men. Now although there be many that are purely conscientious for the use of water-baptism, and bread and wine, we have a great deal of charity for all such; for many that are now joined in society with us, were once as much for the use of these things, as many well-minded people now are; and as the Lord has mercifully brought many of us, in a good degree, to witness the spiritual baptism and supper, we desire that others might be brought to the experience thereof in themselves; and he that witnesses the substance of what many allow, that water-baptism and bread and wine, are outward and visible signs of, is come to the end of the signs; for I hope I may be safe in saying, all signs end

James v. 12.

Mat. vi. 44.

Mat. x. 8

in their substance. Now as we have charity for all them, who do conscientiously use these things, we think they ought to have charity for us, if we disuse them, because we believe they are ceased in point of obligation; and we read that, *Whatsoever is not of faith is sin.* Rom. xiv. 23.

6. CONCERNING PERFECTION.

THIS doctrine of *Perfection* seems very strange and novel, to many that witness but little victory in themselves, over their lusts and passions; and the enemy of man's happiness has persuaded many people to believe, that there is no possibility of overcoming their corruptions and sins, while they are here upon earth, that so they may be quiet and easy in them: or of doing God's will and keeping his commands, that so they may not endeavour for it. Now we believe that God's ways are equal; *is not my way,* saith the Lord, *equal?* Ezek. xviii. 25. God is just in all his doings, and requires no more of men than he gives them ability to perform. If God require that of men which they were not able, neither of themselves, nor by any grace received to perform, then it might be said, that his ways were unequal, and that he was an hard master; but that would be abominable to charge upon the Almighty, who is full of justice and equity. The wise man saith, *fear God and keep his commandments, for this is the whole duty of man.* Eccl. xii. 13. Now if God requires this of men, as to be sure he doth, then there is a possibility of it, or else, as is before observed, his ways are unequal; but it is far from the children of God to charge him with injustice. The disobedient and rebellious people of *Israel* said, that the way of the Lord was not equal; *yet saith the house of* Israel, *the way of the Lord is not equal: O house of* Israel, *are not my ways equal? are not your ways unequal? therefore I will judge you, O house of* Israel, *every one according to his ways, saith the Lord God: repent and turn yourselves from all your transgressions; so iniquity shall not be your ruin.* Now reader, from this thou mayst gather what sort of people they were, that said the way of the Lord was not equal. And we read in the parable of the talents, that it was the unprofitable servant that complained of his Lord; *then he which had received the one talent, came and said, Lord, I knew thee, that thou art an hard man, reaping where thou hast not sown, and gathering where thou hast not strawed.*

<small>Ezek. xviii. 29, 30.</small>

<small>Mat. xxv. 24.</small>

Now we do not read, that the good servants that had improved the talents, complained of their Lord; but we freely own, that no mere man of himself, by his own power, as he is a man, can do the will of God, and keep his commands; yet we believe there is power in that divine grace, that the apostle saith, hath appeared to all men, to enable them to overcome those things which are evil, and do that which is well pleasing to God; *for the grace of God, that bringeth salvation, hath appeared to all men; teaching us, that denying ungodliness and worldly lusts, we should live soberly, righteously and godly in this present world.* Here is both the universality and sufficiency of it, excellently set forth by the apostle; *my grace*, saith the Lord to the apostle, *is sufficient for thee.* Although we

<small>Titus ii. 11.</small>

freely own, that we are weak of ourselves, as men, and cannot of our own power do any thing that is good, as Christ said, *without me ye can do nothing;* yet we say, there is power and sufficiency in the grace of God, to enable men to do his will, and keep his commands, as they take heed unto it; *I am able,* saith the apostle, *through Christ who strengthens me, to do all things.*

It doth not consist with the wisdom of the Holy Ghost, that those gracious promises which are made conditionally upon men's overcoming, and doing the commands of God, should be made if there were no possibility of it; as *He that overcomes, shall* Rev. xxi. 7. *inherit all things, and I will be his God, and he shall be my Son. He that overcometh, the same shall be clo-* Rev. iii. 5. *thed in white raiment, and I will not blot out his name out of the Book of Life, but I will confess him before my Father, and before his Angels. Him that over-* Rev. iii. 12. *cometh will I make a pillar in the temple of my God, and he shall go no more out; and I will write upon him the name of my God, and the name of the City of my God, which is* New Jerusalem, *which cometh down out of Heaven from my God; and I will write upon him my new name. To him that overcometh,* Rev. ii. 17. *will I give to eat of the hidden manna, and will give him a white stone, and in the stone a new name written, which no man knoweth, saving he that receiveth it. He that overcometh shall not be hurt of the second* Rev. ii. 11. *death. Blessed are they that do his commandments,* Rev. xxii. 14. *that they may have a right to the Tree of Life, and may enter in through the gates into the City. To him that* Rev. iii. 21. *overcometh, will I grant to sit with me on my throne, even as I have overcome, and am set down with my Father on his throne. And hereby we do know that we* 1 John ii. 3, 4, *know him, if we keep his commandments. He that* 5, & 6.

saith, *I know him, and keepeth not his commandments, is a liar, and the truth is not in him; but whoso keepeth his word, in him verily is the love of God perfected; hereby know we that we are in him. He that saith, he abideth in him, ought himself also to walk even as he walked.* O that *Christians*, so called, would consider how they ought to walk. It is very unjustifiable to deny perfection, for we read, that

Eph. v. 27, & iv. 11, 12, 13.

Christ came to present the church to God without spot or wrinkle, or any such thing; but that it should be holy and without blemish. And he gave some apostles, and some prophets, and some evangelists, and some pastors, and teachers, for the perfecting of the saints, for the work of the ministry, for the edifying of the body of Christ; till we all come in the unity of the faith, and of the knowledge of the Son of God, unto a perfect man, unto the measure of the stature of the fullness of Christ. And the Scriptures are for the making of the man of God perfect, through faith in

2 Tim. iii. 16. 17.

Christ Jesus. *All Scripture, given by inspiration of God, is profitable for doctrine, for correction, for instruction in righteousness, that the man of God may be thoroughly furnished unto all good works.* And the apostle laboured to present men perfect; speaking of Christ *within, the hope of glory,* he saith,

Col. i. 28:

whom we preach, warning every man, and teaching every man in all wisdom, that we may present every man perfect in Christ Jesus. Why should they teach, and preach for this end, if there was no possibility of attaining it? Yet many have borne hard upon us for asserting such possibility, although it be the doctrine of Christ. If it be but well considered, I think they hold perfection to a great degree, that are called god-fathers, and god-mothers, that do promise and vow three things in the name of a child when it is sprinkled, *viz. That it shall forsake the devil and all his works, the pomps and vanities of this wicked world, with all the sinful lusts of the flesh, and that it shall do God's holy will, and keep his commandments, and walk in the same all the days of its life.* I wish they themselves may be found in the practice of what they here promise for another. It is certain, *Christians* ought to be as like Christ as it's possible for men and women to be, and to walk even as he walked, as far as they are capable.

<small>See the Church of England's Catechism.</small>

He was holy, humble, meek, and merciful; but how much the reverse are too many that profess to be his followers? many who are for imperfection, and say, there is no victory over sin while here, do urge that of the apostle *Paul*, where he saith, *for I know that in me, that is, in my flesh, dwelleth no good thing; for to will is present with me, but how to perform that which is good, I find not; for the good that I would, that I do not, but the evil which I would not that I do.* And verse 21, he saith, *I find then a law, that when I would do good, evil is present with me; for I delight in the law of God, after the inward man; but I see another law in my members, warring against the law of my mind, and bringing me into captivity to the law of sin, which is in my members; O wretched man that I am, who shall deliver me from the body of this death?* If the reader please, he may read the whole chapter through for his own satisfaction: but we may not reasonably suppose this to be the apostle's present state, but rather personating the carnal state of others, or himself before conversion, when he saith, verse 14. *But I am carnal, sold under sin;* for we believe he was in a happy state and condition when he wrote that epistle; as he saith in the

<small>Rom. vii. 18.</small>

<small>Rom. vii. 21, 22, 23, 24.</small>

sixth chapter, verse 2, *how shall we that are dead to sin, live any longer therein?* And in the eighth chapter, verse 1, *there is therefore now no condemnation to them which are in Christ Jesus, who walk not after the flesh, but after the Spirit; for the law of the Spirit of life in Christ Jesus, hath made me free from the law of sin and death.* I wish that all might come to experience these things in themselves. Now reader, if thou wilt observe, although many say, that there is no freedom from sin on this side of the grave, the apostle saith, in the sixth of the same epistle, verse, 22, to the believing *Romans, but now being made free from sin, and become servants to God, ye have your fruit unto holiness, and the end everlasting life.* And *John* saith in his first epistle, *I have written unto you young men, because ye are strong, and the word of God abideth in you, and ye have overcome the wicked one.* May all come to the experience of this in themselves. The apostle *Paul* said to the believing *Colossians, that they were complete in him, which is the head of all principality and power.* The apostle *Peter* told the believers, *that they were a chosen generation, a royal priesthood, an holy nation, a peculiar people, that they might shew forth the praises of him who had called them out of darkness into his marvellous light.* To be sure these did not break the commands of God daily, in thought, word and deed. *We know that the Son of God is come, and has given us an understanding, that we may know him that is true; and we are in him that is true, even in his Son Jesus Christ: this is the true God, and eternal life.* *Behold what manner of love the Father hath bestowed upon us, that we should be called the Sons of God; therefore the world knoweth us not, because it knew him not. Beloved,*

1 John ii. 14.

Col. ii. 10.

1 Pet. ii. 9.

1 John v. 20.

1 John iii. 1, 2. 3, 6, 9.

now are we the Sons of God, and it doth not yet appear what we shall be; but we know that when he shall appear, we shall be like him; for we shall see him as he is. And every man that hath this hope in him, *purifieth himself, even as he is pure. Whosoever abideth in him, sinneth not. Whosoever is born of God, doth not commit sin; for his seed remaineth in him, and he cannot sin, because he is born of God.* It is contrary to the divine nature to sin; and as men are born of it, they will not only know a ceasing from sin, but it will be their pleasure and delight to do the will of God: *Except a man be born again,* John iii. 3. *he cannot see the kingdom of God.* Unless men are born of the divine and heavenly nature, they can never come to do the will of God, nor keep his commands; for it is impossible for men, while they are in the fallen and degenerate state, to do God's will, and walk in his way. We read, *that* Enoch *walked with God;* and before he was translated, the text saith, *he had this testimony, that he pleased God,* Heb. xi. 5. And concerning *Zacharias* and his wife *Elizabeth,* the text says, Luke i. 6. *They were both righteous before God, walking in all the commandments and ordinances of the Lord, blameless.* And that all might take such heed to that divine grace and good Spirit, which God has graciously sent into their hearts, that they might walk in all well-pleasing before him, and in the end have an inheritance amongst them that are sanctified, is my sincere desire.

7. CONCERNING THE RESURRECTION.

BECAUSE we do not hold with a great many people in their gross conceptions concerning the *Resurrection*, therefore some have not stuck to say we deny it; but we believe firmly, that there will be a Resurrection of the just and unjust, and that God will give to every man a reward according to his works, whether they be good or evil; but saith the apostle *Paul, some men will say, how are the dead raised up ; and with what body do they come?* he saith to such a curious enquirer, *thou fool, that which thou sowest is not quickened except it die ; and that which thou sowest, thou sowest not that body that shall be, but bare grain, it may chance of wheat or some other grain ; but God giveth it a body as it hath pleased him, and to every seed his own body. All flesh is not the same flesh ; but there is one kind of flesh of men, another flesh of beasts, another of fishes and another of birds ; there are also celestial bodies, and bodies terrestrial ; but the glory of the celestial is one, and the glory of the terrestrial is another ; there is one glory of the sun, and another glory of the moon, and another the glory of stars; for one star differeth from another star in glory ; so also is the Ressurrection of the dead: it is sown in corruption, it is raised in incorruption ; it is sown in dishonour, it is raised in glory, it is sown in weakness, it is raised in power ; it is sown a natural body, it is raised a spiritual body: there is a natural body and there is a spiritual body.* We believe, if we faithfully serve the Lord while we are here, we shall have such glorified bodies hereafter, as he in his wisdom sees fit, and that satisfies us: but the apostle saith, verse the 50th, that *flesh and blood* *cannot inherit the kingdom of God; neither doth corruption inherit incorruption.* Now what we desire is, that all may know a part in the first Resurrection; *blessed and holy is he that hath a part in the first Resurrection; on such the second death hath no power.* The true *Christians* knew, *That they were passed from death to life, because they loved the brethren:* he, saith the text, *that loveth not his brother, abideth in death: whosoever hateth his brother, is a murderer, and no murderer hath eternal life abiding in him.* And, saith *Paul, she that lives in pleasure, is dead while she liveth.* While men and women remain in a state of death and alienation from the Lord, they are full of envy and wrath one against another; and they live to gratify the lustful desires of the flesh. We read, *that whosoever doth not righteousness, is not of God, neither he that loveth not his brother.* O that all would seriously consider of these things; for it is greatly to be lamented how wide many of the professors of *Christianity* live from the doctrine of Christ and the primitive *Christians*: it is as men come to know the second *Adam,* the Lord from heaven, the quickening Spirit, to quicken them, and make them alive, that they come to love one another as *Christians* ought to do; and if all did but live in the Spirit and doctrine of Christ, they would not only be full of love and good-will one to another, but would also bring forth other holy and good fruits; and they whose fruits are unto holiness, their end will be everlasting life. As men sow in this world, so they may expect to reap in the next. We read,

1 Cor. xv. 50.

Rev xx. 6.

1 John iii. 14, 15.

1 Tim. v. 6.

1 John iii. 10.

that *he that sows to the* Spirit, *shall of the Spirit reap life everlasting ; and he that sows to the flesh, shall of the flesh reap corruption.* Men are not only accountable for gross sins; but we are told by Christ our Lord, that a man must give an account in the day of judgment for every idle word he speaks; and the wise man saith, *God will bring every work to judgment, with every secret thing, whether it be good or evil.* Now we think it not safe for any to be 'too inquisitive how the dead shall be raised, and with what bodies they shall come ; lest that reproof of the apostle, *thou fool,* should belong to them; but let us all endeavour to live as becomes the children of God, that when we leave this world, we may have the comfortable answer of *well done, enter into the kingdom prepared for you from the foundation of the world ;* and all such will know a glorious Resurrection.

4. CONCERNING SWEARING.

WE do not only deny vain, rash and false Swearing, but we also conscientiously refuse to swear in any case, or on any account whatsoever, because we believe that our Saviour, *Mat.* v. 33, 34, 35, 36, 37, did positively forbid all Swearing. For he saith, *again ye have heard, that it hath been said by them of old time, thou shalt not forswear thyself, but shalt perform unto the* Lord *thine oath. But I say unto you,* Swear not at all ; *neither by heaven, for it is God's throne ; nor by the earth, for it is his footstool ; neither by* Jerusalem, *for it is the City of the great King : neither shalt thou swear by thy head, because thou canst not make one hair, white or black. But let your communication be yea, yea; nay, nay; for whatsoever is more than these, cometh of evil.* From which it is very plain, that as they of old allowed true swearing, but forbade forswearing or perjury; so our Saviour here forbids both the *one* and the *other;* declaring, without any exception, that whatsoever is more than *yea, yea; nay, nay;* cometh of evil. As for profane, vain and rash Swearing, it was also forbidden under the law; for the third command saith, *thou* Exod. xx. 7. *shalt not take the name of the Lord thy God in vain, for he will not hold him guiltless that taketh his name in vain.* And as this our conscientious refusal of an oath, in all cases, is grounded upon the express command of Christ, we have great cause to be thankful to the king and government, for their favour, by enacting, that our word, or affirmation, shall pass in cases of evidence, instead of an oath. For many of our elder friends underwent great and grievous sufferings, by fines, confiscations, banishments, and imprisonments to death for this their *Christian* testimony. Swearing is now become so common; that it may with sorrow be observed, that vain and profane Swearing abounds; multitudes in their common conversation, being guilty of it, in open defiance and violation, both of the laws of God and man.

It is very much to be desired, that all who profess themselves to be followers of Christ, may live in subjection to the Spirit of Christ, in themselves, which leads into all truth, and consequently to speak truth on all occasions; men and women under this influence, may be very safely trusted. And it is a reproach to any under the denomination of

Christians, that they cannot be depended upon for the truth of *what they say*. Religion, however, is not yet at so low an ebb, but that there are many honest well-minded people of different professions and persuasions, who have gained so great credit and reputation amongst such as know them, that they are, and can be relied on for the truth of what they write or speak. And were all to live up to the doctrine of Christ, there would be no occasion for Swearing to awe men into true-speaking; for the fear of God, which is a stronger and more forcible tye than any oath that ever can be made, would always oblige and engage them thereunto.

The people called *Quakers* are not the only people principled against Swearing. The *Menonists* in *Holland*, and in the *United Provinces*, they and their ancestors, have for a long series of time constantly refused to take an oath in any case whatsoever; and the *States* have so far indulged them, as to establish, that their word shall pass in evidence, instead of an oath; subjecting them who falsify their words, to the same penalties as those who are guilty of perjury; which we hold to be very just and reasonable. The primitive *Christians* did generally refuse to swear; and it is observable, that when their cruel persecutors sometimes called upon them to swear, they returned this short answer, *I am a Christian*. Divers of the ancient Fathers, and martyrs, and early reformers, were of the same sentiments on this subject; *see Treatise on Oaths;* where the reader will find many weighty reasons against all manner of Swearing, supported by the example and practice of eminent *Christians*, martyrs, and reformers, in divers ages of *Christianity*. And as this subject is thoroughly discussed in that *Trea-*

tise, and a full answer there given to the several objections usually made on this head, the reader will find it well worth his perusal; a few quotations out of which said *Treatise*, transcribed from *William Penn's* works, vol. 1. p. 626, 627, 636, 655, 657, are as follows:

1. POLYCARPUS.*

' The first testimony recorded against Swearing
' after the apostles' times, was that of POLYCAR-
' PUS; who had lived with the apostles, and was
' said to have been a disciple to *John*, not the least
' of the apostles; for at his death, when the go-
' vernor bid him *swear, defy Christ*, &c. he said,
' *fourscore and six years have I served him, yet hath*
' *he never offended me in any thing.* The *Proconsul*
' still urged and said, *Swear by the Fortune of*
' *Cæsar*; to whom *Polycarpus* answerd, *if thou re-*
' *quirest this vain glory, that I protest the fortune of*
' *Cæsar, as thou sayest, feigning thou knowest not who*
' *I am, hear freely,* † *I am a* Christian. This good
' man began his fourscore and sixth year about
' twenty years after *James* wrote, *above all things my*
' *brethren, swear not;* and several years before
' *John* the apostle deceased, for he is called his
' disciple.' See his history and commendations in
Eusebius's Eccl. hist. *Lib. 4. Cap. 15.*

* He suffered martyrdom at Smyrna about the Year 167.
† See the following testimony of Basilides.

2. JUSTIN MARTYR. ‖

Apol. 2. *pro Christianis ad Anton. Pium. Oper.* p. 63.

' It was some time before his suffering, that *Justin Martyr*, who is the first we find writing of it, published an *Apology* for the *Christians* in the year 150, as himself saith; and a second after that, wherein he tells us, after the doctrine of his master, *that we should not swear at all, but always speak the truth.* He (that is Christ) *hath thus commanded,* swear not at all; but let your yea, be yea, and your nay, nay; and what is more than these is of evil.' See his praise and martyrdom in *Eusebius* soon after *Polycarpus.*

3. PONTICUS,* and BLANDINA,

Euseb. Eccles. Hist. *Lib.* 5. *Cap.* 1.

' Under the same emperor, *viz. Antonius Philosophus,* (says *Eusebius*) suffered also *Ponticus* of 15 years of age, and *Blandina* a virgin, with all kind of bitter torments; the tormentors now and then urging them to *swear,* which they constantly refused.'

‖ He was put death at Rome, being scourged, and afterwards beheaded, Anno 168.

* Ponticus, a youth of fifteen years of age, suffered martyrdom, together with Blandina, about the year 177.

4. BASILIDES. †

Euseb. Eccles. Hist. Lib. 6. Cap. 4.

' And in another emperor's reign, *viz. Severus Basilides*, a soldier of authority among the host, being appointed to lead *Peiamiena* to execution, and by her convinced of the truth in Christ, was after a while required to swear, but he affirmed plainly, *it was not lawful for him to swear; for*, said he, *I am a* Christian. He did not lay the unlawfulness upon that oath, but upon *swearing at all*. The history only says, his companions would have him swear upon some occasion or other, not mentioning by what; his answer was, *it is unlawful for me to swear;* and why? *because*, saith he, *I am a* Christian. The consequence is plain, *Christians* took no oaths, therefore not their oaths.'

5. CHRYSOSTOM.

' *Chrysostom* in his days, about the year 398, a man very famous in the church, and therefore stiled the *Golden Doctor*, in his 15th Homily on *Genesis*, saith, *a* Christian *must flee oaths by all means*, hearing the sentence of Christ, which saith, *It was said to them of old, ye shall not forswear, but I say unto you, Swear not at all.* Let none

† He was beheaded at Alexandria about the year 204.

' say therefore, I Swear in a just business: it is
' not lawful to Swear, neither in a just nor unjust
' thing.'

6. The WALDENSES.

' The ancient * *Waldenses,* we have good cause
' to say, denied the taking of any oath in what
' sense the primitive *Christians* and fathers refused,
' and that was *all together;* to be sure their enemies
' charged them with it for above three hundred
' years, and we cannot find that they then denied
' the charge: we suppose none will attempt to
' prove they did, for they were well known in the
' world as to this particular.'

7. JOHN WICKLIFF.

' *John Wickliff,* our countryman, and in his time
' D*ivinity Professor* of *Oxford,* famous for his learn-
' ing and godly courage, in oppugning the doc-
' trines and practice of *Rome,* in the time of *Ed-*
' *ward* the *third,* and *Richard* the *second,* about the
' year 1370, was accused, among other things, for
' maintaining, *that all oaths which be made for any*
' *contract or civil bargain, betwixt man and man,*
' *are unlawful.*'

* About the year 1310.

8. PROTESTANT MARTYRS.

' *John Huss, Jerome* of *Prague, Walter Brute, Wil-*
' *liam Swinderby, William Sawtry, William White,*
  William Thorp, Michael Sadler, and others, who
' suffered death for the *Protestant* cause, are record-
' ed to have refused *all Swearing*, in any case, pub-
' lic or private.'

THE CONCLUSION.

HAVING made the foregoing observations, which are left to the reader's serious consideration, what I greatly desire is, that all may come to the practical part of true religion and *Christianity:* for although a man may believe (according to the Scripture) in God, who created the heavens and the earth, and formed it to be inhabited; see *Isa.* xiv. 18. and also believe, that Christ was conceived by the Holy Ghost, born of the Virgin *Mary*, and that he wrought many wonderful miracles, and suffered death upon the cross, as he was man, for he could not die as he was God; and that he was dead and buried, and rose again, and ascended up to heaven, and that he is also come again by his Spirit into men's hearts: although a man may believe all these great truths, and all the articles of the *Christian* faith; all this will not entitle him to

H

a part in the kingdom of God, unless he comes to live an holy life; for we read, *that without holiness no man shall see the Lord.* *Thou believest,* saith the apostle, *there is one God; thou dost well; the devils also believe and tremble.* *But wilt thou know, O vain man, that faith without works is dead. For as the body without the Spirit is dead, so faith without works is dead.* He saith, *shew me thy faith without thy works, and I will shew thee my faith by my works.* The saints faith gave them victory, and wrought by love, to the purifying of their hearts. The practical part of *Christianity* is too much wanting amongst many of them that profess to be the followers of Christ. *To visit the widow and fatherless in their affliction, and to keep themselves unspotted from the world,* is the religion which will avail men in a dying hour. It is very good for those unto whom the Lord has opened his hand wide, and blesed with a plentiful share of these low things, to be full of bowels of compassion towards them that are in want and distress, and to stand up for the right of the widow and fatherless, this is one part of true *Christianity;* but to wrong and oppress the widow and fatherless, is the reverse of *Christianity;* many, not only amongst us, but, I hope, also among other societies, have so much of the fear of God, that they hate this. The Scripture saith, *that the fear of God is to hate pride and arrogancy, and the evil way.* The more men live in the fear of God, there is the greater hatred in their hearts against ill things; but many for want of this, have fallen into very bad company, and evil things; whereby they have brought great ruin and contempt upon themselves. Bad company has been the overthrow of many. *My son,* saith the wise man, *if sinners entice thee consent thou not.* The enemy of men's happiness doth often make use of ill instruments to draw people into ill things; and as many have been drawn into very wrong and ill things by keeping of loose and bad company, so I believe many have been greatly corrupted, through reading of corrupt and ill books; so that some, from reading of *Atheistical* books, have arrived to a great degree of *Atheism.* But it is very profitable to read the Holy Scriptures, which proceeded from the good Spirit of God, as people read them in the same Spirit from which they did proceed; and there are also a great many other good books, that are written by such as did fear God, which do greatly tend to promote piety and virtue and are very profitable to be read.

Great controversies have been, and yet are among the professors of *Christianity*, about religion: one saith one thing, and another another; so that I believe many well-minded people are at a very great stand to know which is the right way. Now the apostle *Peter*, by the direction of the Holy Ghost, has told us, *that God is no respecter of persons, but in every nation, he that fears God, and works righteousness, is accepted with him.* Acts x. 34 Now here are the terms and conditions clearly laid down, upon which acceptance with God stands; and this is what we desire all people may come to be found in the practice of, that so all bitterness and envy one against another, about religion, might cease and come to an end; that truth and righteousness may flourish in the earth.

If all did but truly live in the fear of God as they ought to do, there would be an holy harmony among the children of men, and love, peace, mercy, truth, justice and equity would abound among them; but for want of this, how doth strife, envy, injustice, and oppression abound, even amongst many of them who profess to be the disciples and followers of Christ. O, that the children of men had but in their own experience, what great reward and peace there is in living in the fear of God, and in keeping of his commands, then they would serve him with pleasure; for there is peace and comfort in obeying and serving the Lord, beyond what any are sensible of, except those that have it in their own experience; so that I believe many pious and good people are thankful beyond what they can express in words, that they were prevailed upon to serve him.

And such are concerned in heart, that others might also be gained upon to serve the Lord, that so they might be truly happy; it is for this end, that many of our religious good friends have travelled from one land and country to another, in hazard of their lives; it is also upon this account, that many have appeared in print; that, if possible, they might be instrumental to gain upon the children of men to fear and serve the Lord; for if men observe a thousand outward observations, if they do not obey the Lord, they will not all render them acceptable in his sight: *Samuel* told *Saul*, that *obedience* was *better than sacrifice, and to hearken to the voice of God*, was *better than the fat of rams*.

When it pleased God to reach to the apostle *Paul*, and bring him to partake of his love and goodness, how did his bowels yearn for his relations and kinsfolks after the flesh, that they might be gained upon to serve the Lord. And his love did not only reach to them, but to mankind universally; for, in his first epistle to *Timothy*, he saith, *I exhort that prayers and intercessions,* &c. 1 Tim. ii. 1. *be made for all men;* and the apostle laboured, as in *Christ's stead, that men might be reconciled to God.* O, 2 Cor. v. 20. what could a true *Christian,* that hath the mind of Christ, go through, that men might be won upon to serve God truly, that so they might experience the love and goodness of God in themselves; for the nature of the love of God is such, that when it prevails in men's hearts, then they desire that others might come to share thereof with them; as the good man of old said, *come taste and see that the Lord* Psal. xxxiv. 8. *is good.* It is when men are truly prevailed upon, by the power of divine love, that they come to be in love with God, and to run the ways of his commands with cheerfulness; for if there were no future rewards and punishments, that peace and comfort which they enjoy, who truly serve the Lord, is very encouraging to them to persevere therein. Friendly reader, if thou believest the death and sufferings of the Lord Jesus Christ, who was crucified without the gates of *Jerusalem,* according as the Holy Scriptures relate, let not this satisfy thee, but be concerned that thou mayest know the Lord to bear rule, and set up his kingdom in thy heart; then will it be easy for thee to do the will of God, and keep his commands. And if thou hast a value and esteem for the Holy Scriptures, do not satisfy thyself with only reading the experiences of the holy men of God, that spake what they were witnesses of, who knew a being washed by the water of regeneration, but seek that thou mayest also come to the experience thereof in thyself. And if thou art conscientious for the outward water-baptism, and bread and wine, be careful thou do not rest in the outward observations, short of that inward and spiritual baptism and communion, which the good *Christians* of old witnessed; that, through the enjoyment thereof, thou mayest grow beyond the use of the outward and visible signs: And as thou findest that some of old knew an overcoming of the enemy of their souls, and received power to become the sons of God, consider what victory thou hast gotten over the enemy in thyself. And as some people have been too inquisitive how the dead should be raised, and with what bodies they should come, let it be thy great concern to know thou art raised out of the grave of sin and iniquity, that thou mayest walk with the Lord in newness of life, and live to his praise and glory whilst thou hast a being here, that so thou mayest attain to the resurrection of the just hereafter.

As the Lord, in his wonderful love and mercy, hath sent the son of his dear love; the Lord Jesus Christ, to die for the children of men, whilst they were enemies to him, I tenderly desire that all may consider the great love of God to them therein, and as he is the fountain and author of all the good that we receive, it is greatly to be desired that his long forbearance, great goodness, and manifold mercies, extended to the children of men, might engage them to care and watchfulness. We read that the long-suffering of God waited in the days of *Noah*, while the Ark was preparing; and when the Lord had long striven with them by his Spirit, and they would not be gained upon, then he destroyed them all, save only eight persons that were in the Ark. It is not long since the pestilence did very much prevail in *France*, by which many thousands were swept away. Now as the Lord has mercifully spared the people of these countries, and the

1 Pet. iii. 20.

Gen. vi. 3, 21. 22.

British Isles adjacent, in lengthening a day of mercy to them; I desire that his great goodness and long forbearance may lead them to repentance and amendment of life; for the Lord, as a tender father, seeks to endear the children of men to himself, by his kindness and love.

And, friendly reader, that thou and all men may be prevailed upon, to walk humbly with God, and live such pious and holy lives, that the great and good end, for which the Lord hath made man, and given him a being upon the earth, to shew forth his praise and glory, may be answered, that thou and they may be happy to all eternity, is the sincere desire of one of the people called *Quakers*

Written at *Amsterdam*, }   BENJAMIN HOLME.
in the Year 1724.

If the reader desires a more full and particular account of our principles, there is an Apology written by ROBERT BARCLAY, which has been printed in *English*, *Latin*, *High* and *Low Dutch*, *French*, *Spanish*, and *Danish*, to which he is referred.

A LETTER

TO THE

REV. NOAH PORTER, D.D.

PASTOR OF THE CONG. CHURCH, FARMINGTON, CON.

ON THE

STATEMENTS OF THE CHRISTIAN SPECTATOR,

IN REFERENCE TO

DR. BELLAMY'S DOCTRINES.

FROM No. XV. OF VIEWS IN THEOLOGY,
FOR NOV. 1834.

NEW-YORK:
JOHN P. HAVEN, 148 NASSAU-STREET,
AMERICAN TRACT SOCIETY'S HOUSE.

1834.

minded men, and that we cannot afford to lose them. We have yet to learn that the Church of Christ does not exist by the wit or will of man, and does not depend for its life and its future on this individual or that, or on any school or sect. The one duty of every body of Christians is to take its position, squarely and immovably, let who will, come or go. Its policy and its faith must not be shaped or directed with reference to persons and parties. It must not give out, or think for a moment, that it lives by suffrage. It must live in God, in God's Christ. *There* must be the hiding of its power. Then will it have large increase, whatever *men* may say or do, But, to be true to our honest thought, we should say that the radical element in our denomination is our element of weakness. It is that which neutralizes all internal effort, and creates distrust and fear without. Its spirituality, if not its ability, is vastly overrated, as the extracts we have quoted sufficiently show. Its spirit and purposes have not been improved by those who have flattered it, in the vain hope to control it and make it a healthy part of the body. The better course would be to show it plainly its errors and offenses, and how much it needs the grace of God, while it should not be permitted, in its unchristian attitude, to dilute the faith, enfeeble the energies, and destroy the life of the denomination.

The great question we are called upon to decide cannot be postponed. It is before us. Management and trick may crowd it out of one meeting, but it will come up in another. It must be met and settled. It will not do to cry "Schism," "Bigotry," "Orthodoxy," "Bondage," or whatever else. We know that we are in a line with the fathers who have gone before us. We stand on the rock which is Christ. We feel that we are right, and we are in earnest. Finally, there are many who are saying, in the words of that venerated and lately departed saint of our communion, Rev. N. L. Frothingham, D.D., "If Liberal Christianity means only an unbounded license of speculation,— recognizing nothing as fixed, admitting any extremes of opinion as the fair results of its free

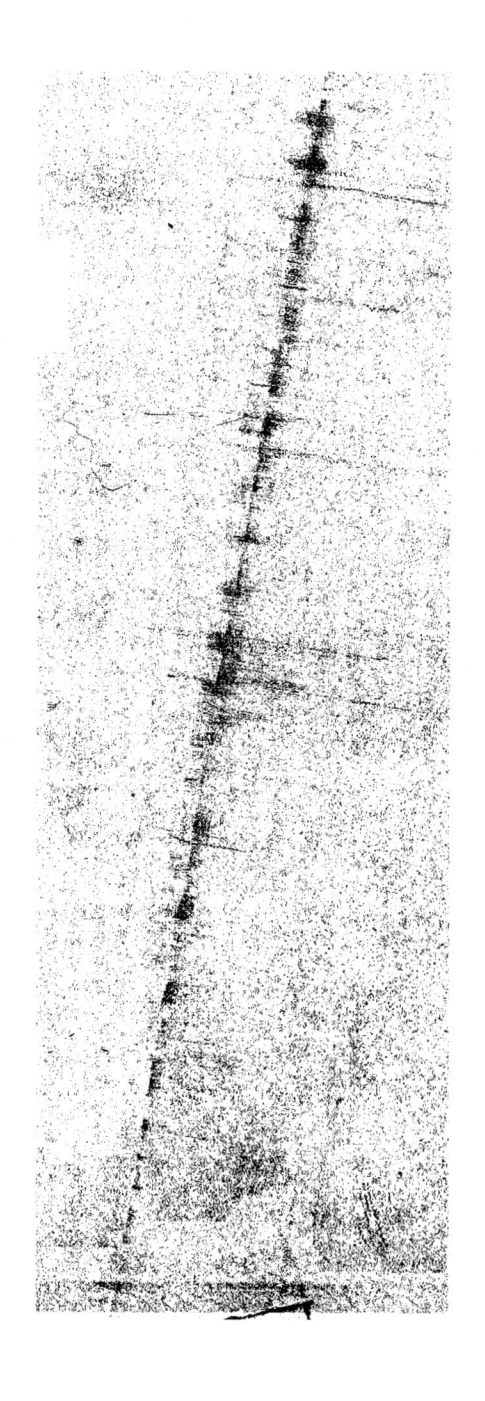